What Turtle Blood Tastes Like

poems by

Jonas Lamb

Finishing Line Press
Georgetown, Kentucky

What Turtle Blood Tastes Like

Copyright © 2025 by Jonas Lamb
ISBN 979-8-89990-160-7 First Edition
All rights reserved under International and Pan-American Copyright Conventions. No part of this book may be reproduced in any manner whatsoever without written permission from the publisher, except in the case of brief quotations embodied in critical articles and reviews.

Publisher: Leah Huete de Maines
Editor: Christen Kincaid
Cover Art: F.W. (Friedrich Wilhelm) Wunder
Author Photo: Courtesy of the author (Jonas Lamb)
Cover Design: Elizabeth Maines McCleavy

Order online: www.finishinglinepress.com
also available on amazon.com

Author inquiries and mail orders:
Finishing Line Press
PO Box 1626
Georgetown, Kentucky 40324
USA

Contents

What Turtle Blood Tastes Like	1
Going Over	2
Her Story	4
When We Were Winged	5
What the Body Remembers	6
View from Right	7
You Saw Me	8
Where God Was	9
Dirt Work	10
Lily Bud	13
Sounding	14
Ways We Connect	15
We Keep the Liquor in the Laundry Room	17
All Under	18
Long-Range Reconnaissance	19
Scale	20
Lesser Devils	23
Wind God	27
Ways to Say Please	28
Timeless	29
Five and Nine	30
Arrival	32
Uncle	33
Deferred Maintenance	35
Prescription	37
What it Was	39
It Matters	41
Night School	42

Snow Dance	43
Keeping Control	45
Undertow	46
On a Kite String	48
[And I like my father]	50
Before You Ask	51
Tree houses, Shipwrecks and Magic	53
Ragged, Loved	55
Ball Jar	56
Kaldūnai	58
Exposure	62
A Roof	63
Brassica Oleracea	65
Fear of Rejection	68
Betting on Long Shots	70
Small Craft Advisory	71
On the Move	72
Anything I can put ketchup on	73
Feared and Afraid	74
Killing Cold	75
Rise	76
Half-Life	77
Notes	80
Acknowledgments	81

*I suspect I am here less for your protection
than you are here for mine, as if you were sent
to call me back into our helpless tribe.*

—John Balaban "Words for my Daughter"

*Bringing children into the world, an act one could argue is
selfish, even foolish, invites trouble. Again, so does poetry.*

—Michael Wiegers "The Poet's Child"

What Turtle Blood Tastes Like

They believed no one could see
them beneath the willow temple,
down by the algae bloom swamp.

They believed if they all drank
of that blood and that swamp water,
they might keep the darkness submerged.

One of their fathers told them,
You can't swim in there shoe-
less, snappers'll get yer toes.

Pike in the night could be heard
when they fell from their brief orbit
through galaxies of mosquitos.

Who was first to lift the rock high?
Who snatched the slick creature from the cool mud
at the brown edge of the water?

They'd been told some kids deserved
a good beating, just as they likely
deserved what they had coming.

From above which boy's head did gravity,
granite and a blow from kids playing
god fall down on mossy diamond shell?

The sound was green wood cracking.
They remember purple blood and sick
tears, the beaked mouth kept on snapping.

When one boy threw the broken
turtle back in the swamp, he became
the one with blood on his hands.

Going Over

Even bird wings, bones porous
as coral, the lightness and flight
nested in honeycomb hollows

are bound to fail and fall. No longer
part of the sky just a tangle
in the grass that chokes

the mower's blades with feather and bone. Beak
and blood. Enough leg left to free from the machine,
and toss into the woods where once

life was different. Into a time
when the woods were an edge
we wanted to fall over—

>into that wellspring
>of mosquitoes, poison
>ivy and leeches, it was our place.
>A place parents didn't go.

>When we went over
>and looked back,
>we saw that we'd
>never really seen

>how big the world could
>be, but we knew how
>to leave it behind
>like a jacket at recess

>and down in the leaf litter,
>scurrying out of the swamp holes,
>we picked skunk cabbage blossoms,
>called them stink bombs

and the trees weren't just trees
they were climbers or sappers
weren't yet birches and pines,
were only hard ribbons of roots

in soft earth hiding
a seam, some slight dip where
a chill and names rose
into daylight,

beech and walnut wind,
willow and sugar maple.
We peeled back birch bark,
to start fires, with the oily paper

skin and pine pitch. Given
space to cuss, fight and piss, to scar
with paintballs, slingshots, pocket knives—
to climb quickly and without caution.

Her Story

Mociute unwrapped
her memories, gold foil
falling away, butterscotching
my sister and me with her hard-sweet
voice, *because we melted, we survived.*
We were amber tough when it was needed,
sweet too when it sufficed,
and we'd seen both sides, the crisp linen
of her blouse, powdered hands,
skin soft over bird-like Baltic bones.

We chewed them like bitter candy,
Mociute's memories, her awkward English.
Though they cast our tiny Midwestern world
into strange light, as years of history
lessons unraveled in an afternoon.

The formal house in Ohio filled with war
and displacement, our inheritance.
In her story, Nazis were the lesser devils, somehow gave
my Grandparents refuge. And they crossed
the Baltic. The Atlantic.

We were dazed by tentative bites
of pickled whitefish with homemade horseradish,
beets and red beans, duck meat and mint jam.
Disoriented by alternative histories
and blurry memory maps.

In *Mociute's* house,
my sister and I became *Laurita* and *Jonukus*—
left the Midwest for Lithuania.

When We Were Winged

we flung ourselves to edges
and over gliding, our scapulae
extended, rigid and feathered.

We flew toward whatever
work and promise might
pay us our worth for this
labor of lifting and traversing
gapped-earth—
gorges, canyons, ravines.

With wings we were quicker
than ferryman, tug or barge.
Less likely to dump our cargo
deep into river, sea or ether.

Winged we were without
our own burden, flight left
us light even when loaded,
circling low to land amidst
wingless dock-hands.

Muscled but meek,
we could see their heavy-hearts
try and lift out of their chests
when we beat our departure
onto the wind and rose.

What the Body Remembers
after Yusef Komunyakaa

Forget what it remembers
instead consider how the body
forgets, or refuses to hold too tightly.

How thin a stretch of silk spans the sky
and connects the spider to the past

a place left behind under last night's hush.
Out to uncover new terrain come morning
when only dew and chill track the path back.

I've forgotten first words, first steps
the moment when letters and white space

between illustrations became words
and more. All of the times that I did not die—
despite the odds, oh how odd I was not trampled

by rhinos along the banks of the Narayani or broken
in a wreck of Jeep—bad tires, puppet string steering

cross town, state lines, countries and borders.
Somehow I've forgotten how lucky

it is to forget. So much these bodies remember,
certain ravages of the deltoid, ear-drum, liver, eyes—

when did that happen? This scar?
I couldn't even begin to tell you.

View from Right

In the swirling dust of shallow right field, I was near enough
to the pop of hard leather on the catcher's softer leather, a little lost
in the smartass static of hey batter chatter, all our cheeks
stuffed with sunflower seeds. Blowing Bazooka bubbles. Coconut

breeze from the first base bleachers where the second baseman's
sixteen-year-old sister tracked the sun instead of our game, and so
didn't see me stealing her signs, squinting at her reddening freckled
chest from the crabgrass outfield, in the company of dandelions.

I watched her and grew dizzy, baking in the Michigan sun, the smell
of lilac laundry soap and glove oil rising off me. She raised a sweaty
bottle of Faygo cola to her lips, lowered painted lashes, ginger hair on
bare shoulders. I was so thirsty. The mercy

rule ended the game early. I watched more girls than I watched ball
games that long summer years before I knew the damage an ineptly
pinned carnation and blood could cause a marigold yellow dress.
Before I learned mascara-tears were harder to clean than grass stains.

You Saw Me

I was a tidepool sculpin, a scurrying
blur among slippery stones, hungry
for the world of light, beyond
the barnacle and bladderwrack.

I was a spined, maligned
and typically tossed-back fish,
aching for some sharp pierce.

A glimpse beyond fin and gill.
And with my parietal eye I sensed you
were a heron,
walking on water,

legs like fragile piers,
golden eye scanning shallows,
tufted feathers at your throat
alive like surf.

Stealth and slack tide,
I might be murk in the blurry margins,
plant or mud or rock,

somehow you saw me
for the fish I was. Ready
for you and your spearing beak
to target the push of my heart,
carry me out of this shallow world.

This is all I longed for
when I was a tidepool sculpin.

Where God Was

I responded, at first, to the call, to the Priest and Deacon, their role
in the deity drama, the congregation, humble, submissive, lifted their
voices into the thick air—heavy wood rafters, blood-colored glass,
the world beyond the church, altered—censer dashed like a weapon
against vice, choking wake of incense, repentance.

Through the doorway tucked behind the altar, robed clergy and altar
boys materialized—I tried to believe—God lurked behind that door,
voice piped-in, angry organ played blind by a Polish seminarian
until one day I stopped singing—stopped feeling any meaning in
the mumbled chorus of the congregation, who did they think was
listening?

Even up close, taking wafer and wine, I couldn't get anywhere close
to knowing why what had once given comfort—conversations with
myself, eyes turned inward, now left me

hollow. Lord? Hear this prayer?

Dirt Work

I

You sent me
        for seeds, I failed
to see you
        meant it was time to dig
deeper, to take root.

While I was away
        you worked the dirt,
your swollen fingers and a rusty shovel
        folded kelp and chum salmon

into the raised beds
        where our seeds
would soon sprout, would transform
        us too. On my scribbled list

even the names sprouted
 origin stories before they were sown

Formanova beets, White Russian
kale, Renegade beans,
Siberian garlic.

When I found you
        in the garden, on your knees
I brought tiny offerings in brown paper
        Each packet, a sort of prayer—
verses of soil temperature, and planting depth.

Propagation.

II

We made dirt
        into dinner. Seeds and sprouts, root deep
                        down dark
                              finger thick, fragrant
when twisted loose to be rinsed and roasted.
So much more summer

than we believed possible.
        Can we can up all this
bounty, before September slugs set in?

We made ourselves kale
        or at least ate enough
to be changed, protein charged, charting.

The two of us, eating for three. Fall turning
into winter, we turned to potato, garlic gnocchi—
        no key
to survival but at least a break from salmon.

        Our calendars force four seasons
onto this wet world
but who are we kidding?
        Transformations mark time, belly
        blossoms, aching back. Seasons
are slippery, unpredictable. Leaf fall bleeding color into early snow.

Only humans could hope for neat seasons, summer
bookended by memorials and celebrations of labor.
Some careful cleaving of a year, like a cantaloupe
quartered and shared.

        That long season of waiting and measuring, we
ate so many potatoes. Cast-iron Dutch oven
stewing chicken thighs, Brussels sprouts.

That season of your sprouting,
Sustained by the labor of our garden. Planting
names now into the air.

Reading seed catalogs, origin
stories of potatoes we hoped
        could root, could hold,
Irish Cobbler, Detroit Red, Holland Longbush.

Lily Bud

This path is a braided way,
through dawn-dark,
salmonberry-tangle and thorn,
from cedar house to mud beach.

In the shade grow chocolate
lilies, *fritillaria affinis*.
Lance-like leaf-whorls and speckled
tepals drip last night's rain.

I remember the midwife
tell me, "the cervix is like a flower."
Like this fetid
wildflower I wonder?

I sit down
on path
beside this lily
beside this greening ground

and I sip tea.
Tea of steeped swollen
flowers, mouth full of mint
and clouds

of hot breath
billow onto
a bowed
brown bud.

If her cervix is like
these lilies,
today our baby
will come.

Sounding

A hummingbird's wings,
a baby's heart, my ear
pressed to her slick belly—
listening.

Ways We Connect

I twist the lid off
so many jars, POP.

Pureed peas
spread across the
small table, the smell
of summer.

The birds of his hands tuck their wings,
bunched fingertips touching thumbs,
come together, connect, plug in,
more.

Then they fly off,
only one hand returns,
to touch five fingers to lips,
again, and again,
eat, eat.

I build bridges
between the small jar
and his wide mouth.
This food, these signs,
a language we share.

His face, now
creamed in green,
his mouth spreads
not-quite speechless.
His hands full of words

flutter up again, *more.*
I reach out and brush
peas from his raised eyebrow.
His gaped mouth follows
my hand on its return
to the spoon. These winter

dark mornings I spoon him summer
while the wings of his hands
touch and dart, *more,*
 more, more.

We Keep the Liquor in the Laundry Room

a crooked porch at the back of the house,
where the dying washer cycles,
bucks and jumps, liquor bottles
on the counter clank and kiss.

The whirl, creak and groan of drive-belt rubbing
a rustic, erotic, mechanical ritual,
tired clutch groping, pump sucking
and the whole house swaying a little,
weak-kneed but strong,
leaning into hard but necessary work.

Load the wash, steal a swig,
extra soap for the shitty diapers,
some Boatright Bourbon or
wash-day white tequila.

We wash it all together on cold.

With two boys, always butt-sliding,
puddle-jumping, kneeling
in muddy gardens murdering slugs,
or in peaty blueberry thickets,
we do laundry almost every day.

So much laundry. Sorting and folding
tiny underpants, wool socks, Carhartts.
Raising solitary toasts to grit.

Watcha doin' back there, Dad?

Lost in a familiar rhythm, lilac bloom of detergent,
some softener for fabric, some for this life.
Cork the Boatwright, set it down slow,

lean hard against the rocking washer,
savor the sound of swaying glass bottles,

Laundry, son.

All Under
after Dylan Thomas

Milk jug warms
on counter, condensing.
Milk-sweat on maple,
cherry, alder, on cutting
board. Poured
milk makes brown
of coffee black.

Under the kitchen, the milk, the Cheerios box,
the boiler boils, burns diesel once burned coal,
certainly soothed wool-wrapped dreamers
waking blurry-eyed on the soft side
of single-pane windows to light coal-black
fires and warm soot-colored coffee.
In this kitchen watched tiny lights
bob on the barely afloat boats
tied to sinking docks
in the windward bay.

Seven blocks above the bay,
yet well-setting below where first light
makes morning-orange over mountains
I pour cereal and milk into favorite
bowls, pack lunches, dry clothes.

Under me, under the kitchen, the fir floor,
cast iron pulse, beast boiler
waking, warming these rooms, where
soon, I must rouse
sleepers from blanketed dream
dens, bundle and battle them doorways
and rainward into the day.

Long-Range Reconnaissance

What is seen is not insignificant
though at such scale and magnification
we likely seem so much less than small.
These bodies, their dark openings

and what is captured when light is let in.

Despite all our ruminations,
our labors—blunt and bizarre
we do not sparkle but blend in
against the backdrop of beaten earth.

Despite its many lenses and complex iris
diaphragm mechanism it fails to see
how we struggle to see beyond ourselves,
our mass myopic outbreak

and the shimmer of our glass hand-held windows.

In all that it sees and stores in its deep memory
of spooled film—high altitude scans,
the devil like details—the fine print
of our text messages and tweets

the profundity of our mobile friendly pornography

it does not see us
not seeing or hearing
the whir of its motor
the hiss of its rollers.

Perhaps we are seen as benign from bird's-eye.

Scale

We're making the world,
        so far only as big as this puzzle

        map of the United States, nearing complete
except we are missing

Rhode Island. All week
        Oscar overturned the house, interrogated the cat, cried.

        There should be fifty pieces he tells me, *why did they make it so small* he demands to know. There have been so many puzzles, so many lost

        pieces. I tell him we might never find it. Suggest we trace and replace it with cardboard, we can even paint it Atlantic blue.

His face says that I am a Dad lacking understanding. My face says I am a kid in P-Town on a whale watching tour watching a very tall and a very small man open

        arms and mouths, they become oceans and a blue whale breaches and I am maybe thirteen instead and puzzled and more concerned over body fat and lean muscle than whales

breaching in the shag ocean of the living room rug. The cat Zeus emerges with Rhode Island in his paws, bats the ocean state into the air and onto the hardwood where it slides, our eyes

        go with it hoping we don't lose it to the black hole under the cast iron radiator. I got it. Rhode Island in hand, it's winter in Alaska and we're piecing back together Oscar's world.

On the map Alaska is floating out in the south Pacific, out of scale and somewhere near Hawaii. I tell him our own hometown, Juneau, is twice as big as Rhode Island, thinking this might help

        somehow with the problem of projection. It doesn't. In his Rhode Island blue eyes he's swimming with dolphins and planting cacao seeds and big island dreams

in this thin Alaskan soil. *Wait*, he tells me. *So where's Juneau?* Now
he's a puzzle, wondering
       how this place, his home, all he knows, though also somehow
tiny, could feel so large.

Some questions are best answered with silence and window gaze.
Oscar finds Florida, Georgia. Alabama panorama, Kentucky is lucky
and laughs.

      I lock two more states
into place, *Virginia and West Virginia.*

He smiles, says, *They're brovers
just like the Norf and Souf Carolina*

where 'Ciute and 'Vukas live!
      Even kids can connect the dots, can find homes for missing
puzzle pieces, empty

spaces. We've united the states, but Oscar wants to know *what's that
yellow on the edges? Were 'Ciute and 'Vukas borned in Souf Carolina or
Michigan or Lifuania? Is this, off the map,*

the rest of the world? What does it mean to live off the edges
      of this map? What else has been left off or lost?

      Canada and Mexico, I tell him are here and here. You have to
start small, close to home. Then you can handle the rest of it.

     Where is Lifuania anyway Dad?
I point at New York harbor

           and sail my finger as far as I can
               into the north Atlantic and over the edge

                  onto the white shag rug and then off

           onto the worn oak hardwood. This nailhead
           right here, I tell him. Lithuania is right about here.

But it's so tiny!

But it's not that small, more like this
        and I uproot West Virginia,
                fly it across an imagined Europe

                          and plant it on the shore
                              of the Baltic Sea.

Lesser Devils

No, the Soviets never sent
my grandparents on the Siberia-bound
trains though they were well-educated,
bilingual and Lithuanian.

The Germans, too had not condemned
my *Mociute* and *Tevukas* as Russian
spies, nor had the *Kaunas*
health sciences campus crumbled
under shells like St. Petersburg had,

so *Tevukas*—only recently declared
Dr. Antonas Azelis, M.D. —insisted with lucidity,
on an emergency appendectomy, but without sedation
for fear of shelling.

———

A hundred miles outside Kaunus, the Red
Army prepared for its second
march to the Baltic.

A meal of canned pork and cabbage,
tin mugs of weak smoky tea.

———

In *Tevukas'* waking surgical
dream, he becomes a dandelion gone
to seed, blown and set adrift, over
wheat and canola fields: watches
so many sickles turn grass and flower
to stubble. Wince of pain rising
through locally anesthetized parts.

Homeland to the east in tatters, under the thin topical
numbness of lignocaine, the hospital
shakes, discharges trusted friends
back into the fray. Some wave
white flags toward surging front.
They greet lesser devils, consider
that one boot on their throat
might be better than another.

―

Iron rails lead to the far Eastern
edge of the continent, some less-certain
darkness amidst swarming black
flies and spruce, some biting death on ice.

With the diseased appendix extracted, *Tevukas*
and *Mociute* crouched hidden together in a car
with no seats, car meant for contraband not passengers.

A hundred kilometers to the border
of Latvia, a hundred more by foot
through black alder, birch and night.
Entire villages cleared by conscription—
Nazis always near.

They limp ragged
into Riga, are greeted as refugees,
offered shelter. And learn to wait.

Ships depart daily. Only arrivals
are news of their sinking.

―

I wonder if *Tevukas*
let anyone see that once-raw
wound, that place where he
let himself be opened.

Before I was *Jonas*, before
my *Mociute* had a daughter who would become
my mother, still new herself to being called *Mamiete*,

she declared herself
Eugenia Liauba Azelis,
boarded the America-bound

USAT General R. L. Howze for boiling seas,
where the Baltic would become
North Atlantic steel.

From Bremen to Brooklyn under care,
of an American captain
who fashioned dream from paper,

his own children far from there.
Uncle Leonas—a toddler
born in exile—sat

at his mother's feet, eyes wide as questions,
following the flight of paper airplanes
thrown from top bunks.

Mociute attended English lessons,
where soldiers called the students
the best-dressed refugees,
gathered them on bottom bunks,
had them repeat
practical phrases:

My children are hungry.
I am a doctor.
I also speak German, Russian and French.
Please, I am a married woman.

Wind God

Once when wind was worshipped, feared
and kneeled before, trees were all hard,

bark wounded, rigid, never rendered a shimmer
of shade. Birds were only birds and never

blurred memories of leaves leaping on stems ends, never variegated
edges, veins flexing, flesh uncertain

as seasons once were. When wind pressed itself hard
against the land, its disciple the rain drove into every fissure,

each weak point in the skin of the earth. Once when green
was spring and fire meant fall, a fury of color masked decay

deep inside, all that was only just born, budding and fearless.

In the church of that once when world, bells high in timbered tower
rang themselves ragged in the gust and gale. Those who kneeled

before the altar of hand-sawn planks, nailed between two bare birches,
they huddled deep in wool blankets, placed shanks of mutton

upon the red wood at the feet of the windward forest. Offerings
wrapped in prayer, each veiled memory, slipped inside

the white down of a cottonwood bud. All that was yielding,
hardened over, a burl, a feather in amber. Fear of stillness,

and of lightness, vulnerable and in danger of the wind's bullying
press. Before wind was divine, there were days so still and warm

and full of birds they were assembled and called summer.

Ways to Say Please

Listen, *Jonukas*

        and I try, strain so my ears and brain
        might make story sense of my *Mociute's* words
        rushing at me in three languages.

        A braided current of code-switch,
        a home before war, when first love,
        and rapeseed fields still bloomed at solstice.

        Before borders opened like revolving doors,
        survival requiring the sense to adapt. To know
        when to say *bitte, pozhaluysta, prashau,*

        a slow river of please, the Nemunas flowing from Kaunas to
        the Curonian lagoon.

When we sailed from Bremen I left
that cursed language behind—speaking German
saved my life—or cursed it, it's difficult to say…

…It served its purpose,
and I remember hoping the next language
life would have me wear

would serve me better
and with less consequence.
We have always been a people

between worlds, and in America,
when I am mistaken for Russian
I close my eyes,

touch this *karoliai gintaris*
my mother gave me, *aš meldžiuosi,*
I pray.

Timeless
    after Jim Harrison

Like you, I'm always trying to fall
away from the measured movement of time,
off calendars, between the hands of clocks.

Am puzzled by the blur of good light
and long thought that stretch out
on the spare sun of January this far north.

Oh, to walk out in the morning
and for it to be enough
for those who love me to know
I will be back,
later…

not by lunch or by dark or dinner,
but later—when enough has become enough
and I've grown tired of the wander of a game
trail or the meander of the wrack line.

To return home and to the thousand
things when the tide says there's no more
beach here, or the moon sets and there's no shimmer
of hoar frost on old snow to light the way.

I'll return, come home,
get to work, play with my boys,
work on the house, get dinner started,
love my wife the way she deserves—
our hands and bodies slip
free from the frame of time.

Five and Nine

[Five]

Five is ready for kindergarten and chess,
for charging down the upper mountain on skis—
for finally getting past four and a half.

Ready always to play, still learning to lose.
Ready for full-contact with his brother, rage
ready but still scared of the fallout. Not ready

to say sorry, far from it. Ready to put on a suit
with suspenders and bow tie. Ready to call it his jazz
man zoot suit. Ready to drum and ready to sing

louder than life, *I don't care
what Mama don't allow,
I'm gonna play my drums anyhow!*

[Nine]

A storm enters the confines
of the kitchen, its windows
loose and single paned
rattle in their frames.

His is the generation
of upsurge, severe turbulence,
squinting, bed-headed boy,
spectacle born to me, less

level-headed, less reserved
and, despite ample warning
something to be reckoned
with if I fail to batten down.

———

Tonight, on stage, he's Zeus
but also, somehow still
my son, red-cheeked and shining.
Thunder god incarnate.

Zeus hasn't come down from Olympus to talk about his father
drama, or about girls—sure, he's a bit girl crazy
lately, but the real reason he's speaking to mortals
is to discuss the FAQs on his Twitter feed.

Zeus Tweets to his mortal
fan base, picks up vegetarian
girls on hikers.com.

But Zeus is also my Finn,
how he's become nine alludes
me, but he's wearing a bed sheet and leather
sandals, is arm in arm with Calisto.

Calisto is his friend and neighbor, starry
eyed for him since she was four, long
before he became Zeus, and made her
a bear to protect her from Hera's wrath.
He can't save Calisto from her son's angry arrow
so, to appease his critics
placed her amongst the stars.

Arrival

Is it the reddening blueberry
bushes pushing tender pink blossoms?

Or the violet crocus
spiking through March snowpack
toward lengthening light?

Perhaps it's in the shock and flood
of a *Pineapple Express* windstorm,
warm rain on corn snow,
a hot blast on our
Southeast Alaskan faces.

Probably it comes with the arrival
of Girl Scout cookies, the tangle
of coconut and caramel

and a Cactus League
radio broadcast riding AM static
and bat crack
through the first open
window since flu season.

Uncle

Paralytic Poliomyelitis, the way it rolled off my mother's tongue,
    could have been Lithuanian, when she whispered,
        "polio from the vaccine." One night I saw

my uncle's shriveled right leg, exposed through the crack
    in the armor of his bedroom door. I'll forget the details
    of his face before I forget the pale skin, the sparse dark hair,

a simple crutch beside the bed. Sweat-stained wood, foam rubber—
    familiar as the nighttime route to the bathroom, lean and hop
    to tiled darkness, relief. Morning, dependable as the backup
    brace, warming embrace

steel and leather, hidden beneath the bed.
    I'll forget his tenor laugh and the nicotine yellow lenses
    of his glasses before shaking the sound of that brace.

Coil and release of springs, pop of destroyed knee joint,
    his stiff way scared us kids when he reached
    for his knee to lock some unseen metal hinge.

Subway trains were his first taste of fast. Deep beneath New York,
    a strange new world. Riding with his mother, emerging
    from the dark tunnel, into light, bridging the Harlem River.

If he could conquer the stairs, he was free, fast as the blue blur
    of an express charging past his stop on the far track.
    Like a flashbulb, those trains, they lit the world in a new light.

In all other light he moved slowly. Slow legs, but quick hands.
    When we visited, we asked him to be the machine.
    Approaching him slow with hesitation, chuckling before

our pressing of his nose activated a blur of arms.
    As the tickle machine, my uncle was too quick for us
    but never fast enough

as a boy to evade the outbreak of fists, sticks and stones
>	of the school yard. In the dirt, under the strain he closed
>	his eyes, imagined he might run

them down, twist their arms until they cried Uncle.
>	Moving to Cleveland eradicated some symptoms, but cruelty
>	cannot be vaccinated against.

As kids we were never fast enough to escape
>	the flashbulb of his cameras when the time would come to
>	pose for the family picture before going home. Though
>	sometimes we moved just enough

to blur. I can see the soft denim faded where pockets
>	squared and stretch over his Marlboros, can see chrome
>	peek out of the garage, the grill of his Oldsmobile 442

When he fired it up, leaned out the window and revved
>	the super duty V8, he was back on those Bronx bound
>	trains, had slipped into a quickening world.

Trains, flashbulbs and muscle cars dilated
>	my uncle's eyes. But fast was, for him, always
>	just out of reach.

Deferred Maintenance

Out back the world is winter-bare
branches of mountain-ash stirring,
redpolls landing, goat's beard
and salmonberry stalks leaning.

A finger of the Pacific,
the coast mountains
and this city clinging between.

But I struggle to stay
focused on that world out there,
beyond these walls, this roof
and the demands of this house.

This crooked, needy centenarian,
its varicose veins of nylon-wrapped wire
meandering through holes bored
with hand drills through rough-cut
old-growth lumber, the wave break
circles of saw kerfs in the grain.

And hidden in the vermiculite,
legacy of Libby, Montana—
sleeps the suppressed memory of the summer
we naively bought this broken house,
began picking its scabs.

In this house I sit to write, listen and
push outward. I try hard to see only
my children riding snowy hills
or picking winter rose-hips
in the park across the street.

But instead can only make lists,
lumber needs for a deck,
linear feet of siding, thinking projects
through backwards, unbuilding to
better see the layers,

until my eyes glaze, my waking
reduced to crudely drawn diagrams
and cut lists.

The feeling that my mind is on its belly,
motion, meaning and music, restricted.
Crawling through low spaces,
below cold rooms, knob and tube nightmares,
rubbing against rotting wood,
rusted cast iron rain.

A boiler built for coal,
burns heating oil now,
at the raging-hot heart of this house,
forces steam into singing radiators.

This soft hiss of steam
a song of sorts, the flawed house
warming on me, my eyes
beginning to turn outward again,
finally grasping the allure
of deferring maintenance.

Prescription

Take risks, every day,
it reads. Dump the Christmas tree
in the woods at the trailhead,

disregard no dumping signs
threatening one thousand dollar
fines. Live a little.

Channel dog energy, microburst
through morning drudgery, riding
on the cresting wave of risk.

All waves must crash, but remember
those waves will stack and build
from shoreline to forever.

A story I heard on the radio,
a mailbox was opened, found
inside a box, its return address:

Lewis Carroll c/o Wonderland,
within the box, a bottle, within
the bottle, a risk, *drink me*.

I ate the scone despite the thick
lemon frosting and the knowledge
of what butter does to human hearts

and a sense of the poppy seeds'
relation to heroin. How many jokes
begin with a *man walks into a psychiatrist's office?*

The doctor writes on his ragged
prescription pad, take two long walks
a microdose of LSD and call me

in the morning. Then we will speak
only of risk, only of climbing out
from dark craters—depressions,

sinkholes. Risk disbelief
that the body, its clumsy grace
in motion is more potent

than drug. Mind altering drug.
Altered minds. Altar of minds.
Altar of body in motion—valves

open and close, replenish and restrict
red river of raging adrenaline, racing
rapids of natural born mania.

A boy on a bike resists braking,
lets gravity and terrain take control.
Balance and instinct, reaction

fear and musculature,
on the saddle of a simple
machine riding a rocky wave.

What it Was

It was a neck massager, it was purple.
It was switchable, as in it had an on/off switch. It was battery powered.
It was a fourth grade Montessori classroom, it was a public school.

It was my son and his friends that brought it there, it was these boys,
it was their laughter and their voices chopped by the vibrating of it,
it was relief, the letting down of tightness in their young neck muscles,

it was the warmth of it, the soft buzzing rubber, it was goosebumps risen.
It was bundled in a grocery bag of garage sale yarn. The yarn
it was musty, it was hidden within and promptly forgotten.

It was fortunate there was a substitute teacher that day, or maybe
It was unfortunate— the sub decided to let this one go.
It was not a stone he would be turning.

It was safe to say their regular teacher would have handled
it with grace. With care, it was certain, she would have known
how to bring the physical and emotional pleasure

it was designed to evoke, to the forefront of the peculiar object.
It was our bodies, she would have said, that deserve to feel good and that
it was nothing to be ashamed of, but it was private and sacred. But

it was a substitute afraid to be honest so their teacher's kindness,
it was something that wasn't given that day.
It was not his teacher, but his mother who helped him understand
what it was. Sugar coating it was not her style.

It was a sex toy, she told him. It was confusion on his face. She told him
it was okay, to touch, to explore, to feel. It would make sense someday.

It was an equation he couldn't calculate. He could make sense of sex—
it was what a penis and a vagina were made to do. But a toy? Was this what it
was meant to do? How could a plaything be a sex thing?

My son found
> it was a hard thing to wrap his head around. He struggled.
> It was a real head-scratcher. It made his headache and so
> it was a reason to stay home from school and to sleep it off.
> It was an excused absence.

It Matters

Round and round, laughter,
footfalls, screams and slammed
doors, *ouch* and *stupid poopy head.*

Saturday morning sounds,
the nine A.M. variety, less muted
than the seven A.M. variety which typically involves
the cello and violin battle, small kids
with instruments, the inevitable
breakage of fragile objects.

If I can get coffee before
the first scream, before the first
Mommy call echoes through
the house, then I am only
slightly more ready

to face the uphill climb
of a day of parenting.

My wife, bless her heart,
insists I'm not enough involved,
a spectator really, an anxious one
at that and she's right, yet

I couldn't face it
day in, day out with-
out knowing how much
it matters, this measured chaos,

Monopoly games at six in the morning,
Pokémon Go walks in sideways rain,
the need to comfort a fallen and bruised
boy, yet again with the kind of healing

touch only I can bring, despite
my disconnection, my lack
of first-aid training, somehow I

can be all that these boys need, some-
how an equilibrium is reached.

Night School

I
lie.
I mean
the other kind,
lay. I want to know
how to lay beside my children.
Not merely beside, but close and tender enough to feel,
this is what dads do. Put my nose in their hair, smell the way they
move through water, light. No more bristling when our cold bare skin
connects. All my attempts, gestures, prayers, give them less warmth
than my cradled arm beneath their sleeping heads.

Where
should
I put
this heavy
handed arm of mine?
Here? Can he even raise his ribs
under the weight of my over-thought, calculated
tenderness? I pretend my touch will steady his ragged breathing, repel
his nightmares.

There is
no wrong
way to hold
these children tonight.
Hypnotized by my voice, the smell of paper, light touch of reading
lamp, a softness I'm circling, less awkward, more nature than nurture.
Some nights they reach out and hold me, will not let go. I try not to
memorize the placement of their hands on my body, but instead feel
the need, not the weight. I've got a lot to learn.

Snow Dance

We ask the sky
if it remembers snow.

It is mute, darkening—
leaning in to hear the voices,
of a man and his sons.

How do we snow dance, Dad?
    Yeah, this hill needs some snow for sledding
    and angel making!

Arms up, fingers spread
to tickle the scowl
from the clouds,

like this, I signal the boys,
I twirl, I tickle, I sing—badly,
Let it snow, let it snow, let it snow.

My boys mirror me, lift
their arms, twirl, tickle, and sing. Oscar says,
I know the sky will be laughing snow now!

Overhead, cottonwoods are watchmen.
They shiver limbs, last yellow
leaves tumble. Fickle afternoon

light, lost behind grey mountains
and at the bottom of this hilltop town
the ocean, sable, still.

We hold our arms high
waiting to catch what is let down.

Bruised clouds being to lighten,
sky at last—begins to laugh.

Our feet make small circles
on the frozen ground, our hands
conduct ritual tickling—

Night settles. Down-
soft flakes, snow on our faces.

Keeping Control

Son, our human bodies are time-bombs. All around us, family, friends—
detonating even if our own body-bombs have years left on the clock,

we are full of destructive potential and shrapnel. Hope in God
has been scientifically proven to be less effective than a placebo

in the control group. Even less effective against shrapnel, though I keep
this from you. No one is in control. I appreciate your belief in me

as your father, but believe me when I tell you that my control over you
is tenuous. I am in complete control, complete control of very little

other than the dog or cat and really, I rarely have any control of them or
myself for that matter. After all who wants to be in control? Control

is a cage for responsibility, though I keep this from you. Some days I hear
my own time-bomb ticking furiously. I lose track of time every day.

Responsibility is always knowing what day it is when you ask. Time
management is an essential survival skill but will do very little to keep

the time in the bomb managed, keep it from marching on, expiring.
To explode is to relinquish control. I fear exploding, so feign

control, though I keep this from you. I hope I'm not in the control group.
This look on my face is me showing you what control should look like.

Undertow

When I say *I am sleeping*
I mean I am slipping
and a shore is not unlike a bed
and the undertow drawing me deeper
is not unlike the sweat of a breathless dream.

When I say *I am working*
I mean I am wondering
and the work of following the thread of a thought
wondering its way to the edge of my head
at the end of the day is hard!

When I am working
with wonder I'm rarely ever done.

> I may say *I am done,*
> but I really mean I am doing all I can.

When I say *I am ambitious*
I mean I am anxious, ever so anxious
about slipping and sleeping,
working and wondering,
doing and done.

When I say *I am,*
really I am always enroute
to tomorrow or next Tuesday,
instead of here, in this house,

in this focused light.

When I say *I am living*
I mean I am learning
and learning is not unlike hiding
from what I already know
and hiding is not unlike walking
right up to the banker and turning out empty pockets
or to the teacher and shaking out blurry verse.

When I say *I'm a Dad* I mean I'm
playing catch, and catch-up, putting on band-aids,
trying not to curse too much, drinking lots of beer.
When I say *I'm a Dad* I mean I'm bound
to my pack. I'm growing gray, and fabricating
fictions for my boys and for myself every day.

When I say *I am concluding*
what I mean is I am conducting

      a symphony which is not unlike a tsunami

and the cellos are not unlike a soaring warning siren suggesting high ground, and by high ground I mean a vantage point for viewing the crash that comes at the end.

On a Kite String

This   poem   and   this   dying
dog and my they-look-just-like-you
boys. Their waking and their vitamins.

Their rice krispies and raisin bagels, their Magic
Treehouse and Olympians and their bedtimes.
Dying   dog   and   his— our— my—   pills.

The dog's pills and my addiction,
in his cataract mirrors I see
and hate myself for blaming the dog.

Cocktail of shame, hope, just
die   dog,   die.

And the joy of dog walks even though I'm walking
a dying dog on failing legs. That pained tail
tuck and then the vomit pile,

kibble and pills,
this anxiety, this poem.

This secret need to swerve, highly functional
addict, reckless. High at breakfast,
blurry   commutes   on   stud-rutted   roads.

The dying dog and his eyes,
growing rounder and hollower
each dulling day. The dog and his daily

meds, two buttered up tramadol. One for me so I could see
through   world   blur   and   empty, wet   eyes,
sent up on a kite-string all day.

How I   blurred and softened   hard   edges
believed the smell of morning
sea fog, the sound of my son's cello,
cup of coffee and a kiss from my wife

were not enough. Beach barbecues and knee
high rye grass hiss. Kids leaping
creeks, topping boots and building fires.
I   cracked   and vanished so many   sweaty beers,
roasted hot
dogs and salmon on coals. Sunset on snow
caps. Why wasn't this enough?

Big white peaks edge into sky, little white caps roughen the water,
little   white   pills   in   my   pocket, in me,   in the ashes
of dog taken away on the wind.

[And I like my father]

And I, like my father
have raised children and bottles,
bourbon and breast milk, though not formula, but, like him, I am fallible. Forever
pressing up against Peter and Neverland.

      Repulsed by responsibility and compulsively,
repulsively, hitched to this place, these children, these heart, bone and want houses,
        these mortgages, emotional and otherwise.

And I, like my father
      only rarely

have slept on the couch after too much raising
of children and bottles and Cain. Love is eating
thoughts, words. Is taking back what is spit in *I don't want to grow up!*
fits.

Never near when needed, and *just go, please.* A part of me, like my father
      too much to handle, and why
      handle what's broken
      with care anyway?

Before You Ask

> *I don't even know how to match my socks.*
> *Go ask your mother.* She laughs and says,
> *I did. Mom told me to come and ask you.*
>   —Joe Mills "How You Know"

Son, you are likely to think
this life is a puzzle, with so many missing
pieces, so you should know who to turn to
when nothing fits together.

Your mother will be straight
with you as certain as I will be half
listening and reluctant. Before you doubt
this remember when you were eight

she laid the words, *vagina*,
penis and *vibrator* on you? Remember
just last night how hard you laughed when your little
brother asked if babies came out of butt cracks

and how your mother clarified for him the map
of a woman's underside, *vulva, urethra, vagina, perineum, anus*.
How his nose wrinkled and one eyebrow raised as he began to put
together the pieces. Realize his kindergarten teacher was pregnant,
thought how does that work?

So before you ask me about what causes depression or your grandpa
about his weight or his heart, consider whether you want stories
or if you want answers? I don't mean to say stories never end
with answers, but the answers come quicker when you ask your
mother

instead. She won't hesitate to tell you how dark winter gets,
how the lack of light and stress of work and you kids can make brains
back-fire. She'll cut quick through grandpa's shit, tell you straight that
he's too heavy—that his heart is failing and he's not getting enough
oxygen so his brain too is getting slow.

Your mother wants to arm you
with truth. Prepare you—I guess. Which
isn't to say that what I want for you is fiction
but I'm afraid you know too much already

and maybe not ready to face the worst
of this world, not yet. You're a smart kid
and will probably find a way to side-step
some of the gut-punches on the way.

So let's go back to what I said
about your mother. Before
you go ask her, ask yourself
if you're ready to know.

Tree houses, Shipwrecks and Magic

A moment alone, living room emptied of life, growing still.
First house, first starry-eyed moments of the new year
King Julian, bless his meerkat heart, granted us a gift—
a New Year countdown on demand. So at 9:30 we hid

all the clocks in the first house, starry-eyed, nearing a new year
a five-minute dance party and then all the kids sent to bed
the New Year counted already down and hidden by 9:30
pumpkin pie and bedtime-sounds spill out from oven and under doors.

Our five-minute dance party, stilled and settled, all the kids in bed
hushed crinkle of turning pages, touching licked fingertips to paper
pumpkin pie and bedtime-sounds slip beneath the bedroom door.
With murmured voices, dream seed stories are given.

Hush and hear crinkle of paper, fingertips licked, pages turn
and tree houses, shipwrecks and magic, these kids not yet
tired of murmured voices dream seeding stories
not yet too old or cool to wear zip up pajamas.

Tree houses, shipwrecks and magic, these kids not yet
ready to take the needle-bare Christmas tree down
not yet. Zip up pajamas are still cool, never too old
to believe Santa flies a floatplane, a sack load of new skis in back.

I was the only one ready to take down the Sitka Spruce
Finn called the training tree. The neighbors laughed, Oscar yelled,
Santa flies a floatplane, he's bringing new skis!
Yelled ouch every time he got too close to the bright, blinking tree.

Finn called it the training tree and we laughed. At the neighbors
my wife drank wine with the wives, their husbands, gone hunting caribou.
Oscar hollered every time got too close. Bright, blinking tree,
dream seed stories falling with murmured voices down the stairs.

My wife next door drinking. The other wives' husbands gone.
This house full of kids, some of them mine, all of them, now sleeping,
their dreams seeded with stories told with murmured voices.
My brother-in-law's voice crosses the continent on the line,

this house full of kids, some of them mine, all of them, now sleeping
through their cousin's arrival at 11:30, *her name is Fallon Elizabeth.*
From across the continent, my brother-in-law, becoming a father,
Wives next door drinking wine—their husbands out hunting caribou.

My niece, Fallon born minutes before midnight
a voice reaches across this state into the line next door, a father
a caribou hunter, says *goodnight.* Next door his wife tells him, *kill
something tomorrow for me, babe.* Adak and Juneau a whisper away.

Ragged, Loved

1
Though we knew little of Oscar Jasper Brenton; encyclopedia salesman, seasonal gypsy of the Midwest territory, a drunk, womanizer, loved by his sons who fished every muddy river from Iron Mountain to Oshkosh, trout lines and Kiekhaefer Mercury outboards, we named our second son after him and some Dubliner. Oscar Wilde Lamb, the shock and the joy of his arrival. Windows drawn December dark by early afternoon, steamed on the inside, kettle breathing on the woodstove. Our first son glowing, ski-tired, held out the handmade card toward the tub, his brother's hot body bloomed into winter.

2
At age two, Oscar, the finally sleeping child, warm and blanketed deep on couch Jack-in-the-boxes when the movie ends. Credits roll and dance party exit music has his mom and brother shaking it on the living room rug. I'm numb and dumb and nearing peace, but now he's up, eyes closed, he's whip and nae-naeing, bop and stanky-legging, his lips moving but in a rare moment, he's quiet. Lip-syncing, ooh watch me, watch me. And then zombie arms reaching, sightless but sensing mom's proximity. TV off now, mom scoops sleep dancer, we all ascend stairs, slowly, ragged, bedways.

3
Oscar insists the second-hand, mangled book is not a Pirate's Log but a secret journal for summer adventures to faraway worlds—Haines, Glacier Bay and the Yukon. Forget the pirate name generator he demands we get down to the business, dictates *Day 1: Epic Jousting.* Begin with inflatable weapons, boxer's headgear and his older brother balanced on wobbly pedestals. In the inflatable ring, a moment of kindness makes them equally matched, round after round they batter brother heads but do not break. They are five and ten and knock me sideways daily. I stand smiling as they attack. For a moment, maybe I'm not even on edge. For now the brother battle is all tied up, two knockdowns a piece. At the strong-man game the barker calls *seven* ding *eight* ding *nine*. The boys swing, laugh and scream, cheer the strongman swinging a sledge, pounding the earth to raise a tiny steel ball, hoping to ring song from bronze bell. Three thousand days as a parent. Tiny triumphs crystalize and blur.

Ball Jar

Drawers, jars, racks
hands and fingers,
lid, mouth, lip, metal.

Seals and countertops,
clank, song, glass,
empty vessel and its dreams.

Full dreams, half-full dreams,
fresh, rancid, crisp
cucumber, vinegar, pickle.

Lid off, summer in.
Dirt, peat and seaweed in.
Water too, from rain, from well
in jar, in radish and beet,
cabbage and purple carrot,
all of it in, seed, root, stalk
and greens, all in.

Midnight sun, salmon,
memory, rain music on roof
also in, poems too,
pickled for later.

Vinegar and pressure,
gasket rubber, red as beet
stain on handling hand.

Dill, salt, turmeric,
little jars, red lids,
green labels.

Drawer full of herbs
in jars, selfish jars,
secreted fragrances,
flowers from far away.

Autumn sea of purple
crocuses opening, harvested
and dried in dog day sun,
from the flowers, glean saffron
threads to scent and color cream,
savory curry sauce sweet on tongue.

A tall black beer poured
from bottle to pint jar
to mouth.

A candle in a jar
softly smoking light inside,
wax run, wick, a room,
less dark.

Dinner and done,
beer and bottle and jar
empty, a different drawer,
containers for leftovers,
jars, like bass
smallmouth, largemouth,
one once for peanut butter,
another, for peonies at Easter,
tomato sauce, couscous,
an ounce of mouth-watering
marijuana.

Jars for today,
jars for tomorrow,
places for poems
to age, savor and save.

Kaldūnai

Three, one, one,
says my Mom,

guiding me though
I'm in a different kitchen
now and on my own.

———

Three cups flour,
one cup water,
one egg.

Knead together
adding water
one tablespoon
at a time.

*Don't let it get
too sticky.*

Roll the dough
until an eighth of an inch
thick and cut

into rounds using the rim
of a small juice glass.

Put on a large pot to boil
and sauté three to four cups
of mushrooms in butter.

Look for wild varieties
at the market, if available
or better yet go into the forest.

———

Look for the *baravykas*—king bolete
voveraitė—little squirrel
or *lepeška*—yellow chanterelle.

Pretend it's midsummer in Lithuania
nearing *Rasos*—the dew holiday.
You are dressed in handwoven linen,
draped in a sash ending in tassels.

Kneeling to pick mushrooms,
your ancestors swarm and braid
through Poplars.

Into moonlit meadow
wearing garlands of wildflowers,
eating cucumbers dipped in honey.

A bonfire and *kupole*—maypole await,
dancing and drinking *Krupnikas*—
smaller fires flank the flurry of swirling white linen,
guide the rising sun home to the shores of the Baltic.

———

Imagine it is morning now,
Jonines—St. John's Day,
your name day, the dew heavy
on wheat fields, frogs and belladonna.

Imagine you are reborn
in a different time, on a different shore.
Your dead grandparents and this old world
are not dead, are not torn by war.

Lietuva and *Mociute* and *Tevukas*
are alive and their world is new,
is fresh, like these mushrooms,
these fragments of a language
opened up like a paper-wrapped gift.

―

The bite of horseradish
and pickled whitefish,
memories of the nose,
the mysterious *Kucious*—Christmas feast
spread out on a linen tablecloth.

Next to the laden table,
on the dining room wall, a painting
of the farm and pasture that was their home

a time before the wars.
Before the Germans
and the Russians,
before my Mother
and Father. Before me.

―

But remember
the mushrooms
the *baravykas*,
voveraitė and *lepeška*.

Place your treasures
in a paper sack.

Or better yet, wrap them in a handkerchief
that used to belong to *Tevukas*.

―

Drop in the *kaldūnai*
one by one, stirring
so the dough doesn't stick
to the bottom of the big pot
breathing steam up into your face
and filling the kitchen
with so much more.

From the small radio in the breakfast
room WJCU Cleveland plays Lithuanian
news and Strauss through soft static.

We called it the breakfast room
just large enough for the table, six chairs
and little else but the stand on which sat the radio
bringing a distant world into ours.

———

How often I snuck cookies
from the cool ceramic belly
of the Cheshire cat cookie jar
when *Mociute* turned to the stove.

I sat in a chrome-legged stool with black vinyl seat
in her kitchen, listening carefully, when my siblings wouldn't.

Even through heavy accents and broken
English, her stories kept me close while she cooked.

I listened and I watched and I hope
she will someday forgive me,
from her place in *dangu*, for making *kaldūnai*
for a Russian potluck and for calling them *palmeni*.

Exposure

Our hundred-year-old house leans toward what openings
can be found between adjacent structures stacked three-deep, rising
up the steep hillside from the sea.

Our house is level but not plumb. Its cedar skin sheds
paint, has waited years for some loving touch, to be scraped, to be
painted. We hope the next sunny days might warm the wood enough
to dry the perpetual damp.

We cross our fingers for one good summer in five to run the power
washer and go up on the roof and nail down new zinc strips, keep the
moss at bay. Exposure wears on this broken-down house, this life on
the cold, remote coast, everything leaning

south for good exposure. But the storms roll in that way too, Taku
winds bombard while we lean in, long for the sun's soft touch instead
of gut-punch gale. At three in the afternoon the house is a lantern in
the December dark, the glowing windows a wash

of amber light. Despite renovation, inside we fight the chill, draw
blinds to hide the drizzle that blurs the windows, refuses to freeze. We
teach our kids to tent the kindling in the woodstove, strike the match,
make a fire. By warm lamp light we play rummy, listen

to news on the radio and worry after faraway friends occupying
other cold coasts, in Norway, Antarctica. Wonder what they turn to
for shelter against exposure, what light sustains them. From what
darkness and doubt their storms are born?

A Roof

I finish the new deck roof,
rough-cut yellow cedar
under clear polycarbonate panels
so I can watch the falls
of Mt. Juneau, grill salmon
out of the rain.

All night, sky unloads, wind
gusts forty, tests the work of my hands,
my calculating mind.

Under cover
of sleep's light roof
  and heavy clouds,
    I wake and roll
     each time the tired chimney braces
  against the heart of this house,
  an uneasy song of joists & stair stringers flexing.

I turn from window draft,
  toward bed's warm center,
    doubt my efforts,
certain my shoring up
  of this old shingled ship,
    will founder.

I try to hold together
    my thoughts, my breath.
     Hoping it might be enough
    to keep this house, this family, this life,
     sheltered & sturdy.

I sweat through sheets,
  am as tired as
    the flags atop the Capitol
     are wind-thinned.

Wind chime, in the bare lilac branches,
    swirls in each gust, rings out,
        at this hour, in this storm, its song
            is not soothing.

I doubt these hands, this house,
    this life, yet the storm blows North,
        somehow the center holds.

Day is a brightening room, and breakfast,
        bagels and eggs for my boys,
    they eat, tell me thanks, even.
    The espresso roast I grind and brew is dark and delicate.

I step out the back door to confirm
        the roof has held.
The night's rain and wind are a dream
    that I'll forget once I leave the house.

Brassica Oleracea

      1
Brussels sprout, *Brassica oleracea*—
wild cabbage I could never stomach
until my two-year-old son,
Oscar Wilde, demanded more
Brussels, Dad.

A snack time experiment
I roasted the tender buds
in our ornery oven
halved with a paring knife
lightly oiled and salted
,

      2
Four now, Oscar smirks
through a mouthful of soft, toasted sprouts
whenever I make them. Always wants to help cut
them up, small hands, small knife
dash the salt, open the oven.

Remember Dad,
how I teached you to love
Brussels?

      3
After dinner we pop
the top of the steamy
seed-starter box.

See those sprouts? I ask
our faces come so close
I can smell Brussels on his breath.

Are those gonna grow into big Brussels?
His widening pupils are wild
cabbages blooming.

4
I remember the freezer burned
green giant smiling on the side bagged
beans and broccoli growing
hoar frost in the freezer
then went limp
in the steamer.

Never, I tell Oscar;
that's how many times
I ate Brussels sprouts
before now.

Nothing so savory, tender
and buttery as these Brussels sprout
buds came from my childhood kitchen.

5
All summer we watered
and watched the violet heads unfold
bolt upright, the thick stalks
begin to speckle with buds.

His small hands aren't strong
enough yet to pinch and twist the sprouts
from the stalks, he races toward the house
I'm going to get a knife, Dad, be right back.

Just wait, I tell him. *They'll come
off easy when they're ready.* We wait
weed the rows, pull carrots, can sense
by their thickness, that fall is near.

As the nights cool and the wind picks up,
we uncover the garden for the harvest—
only the kale is tough enough for what's coming.
Brussels sprouts surrender to our fingers

bounty plunked into the colander.
Before we take them inside to roast
we tarp over the tilled soil, tie down
what is light, until snow sets its wet anchor.

Fear of Rejection

Breathing is optional
in dreams. Waking is eventually
necessary, though can prove challenging.
Real waking that is which differs from dream
waking, trying to shake sleep, to open lithium-lidded eyes
onto awareness of the dream, seeing the lines of code.

Recognizing some familiarity, recalling Mom's voice
weak and breathless on the phone as she translated
a study she read in a medical journal, now she is optimistic
but even asleep I think she is naive, her hope
a clinical trial. The control group is uninformed,
certainly not in control. I wonder who has more

power to save, the donors or pulmonologists?
To dream is to have hope, this is an accepted paradigm.
But this is only a dream, a thing that can be rejected.
God is on one side of a flimsy curtain or maybe two-way glass
checking in on the transplant ward. The outlook is fuzzy,
dreams are made of the same gauzy material.

Waking while dreaming won't shatter
white tiled medical lab where we are together
with Mom, hanging on hope, fearing rejection, shatter
resistant, refusing to wake. We are peering into the lab
where empty yet animate Tyvek suits and latex gloves
tend to their gardens. Growing disembodied lungs—

hydroponics of course, dirt is unsterile. So fertile
these dreams, two budding lungs bloom fuchsia
drooping lobes pulse at the ends of each bronchus
branch. Roots in fluid sway unrooted, in suspension,
bronchioles, florets, immunosuppressants, lung tissue
tended to with tenderness, nutrient supplements, faith.

A fully ripened pair is clipped and extracted from its glass
terrarium, planted into the warm incubator wrapped in a cage
of raw ribs. The synthetic heart is vital to circulation,
the aquarium glass, the lavender soap, the clean room
merely minimize exposures. Procure premium donors,
garden heirloom varietals, organs, body parts, parts of this dream.

Parts of me may be secretly germinating
the seeds of familial fibrosis. A haunting inheritance.

Hold on a while longer, Mom. Steady now, oxygen
concentrator, green bottled breath on wheels, diffusion
of oxygen through alveolar wall, cellular divide between life
& dream & an engineered lung longing to be real
to be filled with heat, with heart pumped blood.
Beyond the sterile lab, beyond swinging hospital

doors open on the dirty world, Mom waits with canned oxygen,
considering cryogenic sleep, a way to opt-out of waking,
bronchoscopy, respiratory therapy and other bodily invasions
until her new parts are ripe & ready for harvest. I wake
wondering when a donor will die, when one dream
ends and another begins.

Betting on Long Shots

Don't begin with the delicate
such pretty objects never hold
up to all the hardness
that will knock up against us.

Begin, please, with the hard—
the unbreakable, the titanium
which yields and bends but always snaps
back, despite how difficult.

Begin knowing organ transplants
are longshots, are hard horses
to bet on despite how hard we hope
for miracles in small packages—

jockeys in tights and boots
the sharpness of their heels
spurring horses, rise of ribs
blur of hooves and dirt track.

Cells in lung tissue attempt
to smuggle oxygen across borders—seek
asylum. To be carried on swift rivers.
To turn blood red.

Despite the temptation to believe
in miracles, resist—
these delicate dreams are endangered
as are winters with snow.

Start here instead—
bodies fail, parts stiffen. Parents too—
their hardness certainly will soften
but know also, their softening will harden us.

Small Craft Advisory

We were all more or less
        falling. And that's all we wanted.

So much gravity leaning
        hard against these scaffolds of bone

        and how they refused to break or bend,
or become holy or hollow enough

to fall with grace, sway
        of a swell-tossed boat, swamped

        and each time rising from trough
to peak, arc and fall, soaked and salted

seething and alive.

On the Move

Through morning,
aspen's silver seashells still.

Animals moving,
Fleet with fear, supple, strong.

Man, moose and beaver.
So much more than heartbeats complicated.

Heron wings toss light,
beak extracts eel from lake shallows.

Mallard moves water,
kicks ripples, ripples sky.

Forest canopy leans lakewards,
leaf-shadows walk on water.

Beaver brings down birch,
builds den, a between place.

Den hovers, floats, full of food,
refusing pond and shore and winter.

Beaver will fight for kits, kill
swimming dogs fetching thrown sticks.

Anything I can put ketchup on

To call them berries
really is blasphemy—
too bitter without
help of cinnamon, cloves, molasses.

These cranberries
hanging in frosted bunches
bagged to be boiled
milled and canned.

This collecting,
this pushing through dense brush
down grown over logging roads,
and this speaking of the words
hey
and
bear.

This balancing act
of supermarket and
backyard.
These berries,
this ketchup
they became.

This hunger
for anything I can put ketchup on.

Feared and Afraid

Bear is bear, man
longs to return to animal
self, to wake lean muscle,
and remember a time when to run
meant to survive.

Forest is forest, bear longs
to be bear, gorging on dandelion
greens in the cool alder shade,
nosing cubs to nurse, or steering
them to safety of higher trees
each time jet engines thrust
on a nearby runway, aluminum skin
reflecting fish scales of sun.

Summer's first salmonberries
collect in paws and hands alike,
cubs and kids yawn, paved ways braid
through what remains of wild
spaces, our circles and territories intersect.
Probability and logic, two legs or four.
They eat and are eaten.

Man runs nightly through never night
of Anchorage summer, wilderness pushes
back against the order of the city,
against the food chain.

Bear eats, man eats,
bear kills man kills bear.
They are feared and afraid.
At the center of both,
salmon and berries.

Killing Cold

My cat, Zeus does not mind a New Year's arrival though despises
the fireworks signaling some newness, some beginning in the foggy
night, too warm for January in Alaska, for cats, dogs or other fur
bearing mammals.

Bombogenesis, Fire and Fury, glare ice on the Kuskokwim, open
water, five survivors, father fallen, gone under, fished out of the river
with hooks on New Year's Day & in Florida, iguanas fall from night
roosts, flash frozen, though likely, as they warm up—

come back to life. Thresher sharks turned sharksicles
littered Cape Cod beaches. This new year too cold for the cold-blooded, though just right for killing invasive species; Burmese pythons in
South Florida, two homeless Houston men.

Rise

To get out
        of the deep, first
go down—

work that furious club-tail
through tunnel twists,
down, then up, then out.

Out of the deep-den,
        beaver through waking,
through mist music,
light deep like black spruce
down at roots but rising.

Brittle sap-floored forest,
so many needles dropping,
daylight falling but trapped
in drooping night-net.

Rise, emerge,
        from den
and water warp, where sight
swarms, blurry forest and fractured light
        come into focus,
        membranous inner-eyelids
        lift.

Swim beaver, wet still,
become day, walk now,
spit spruce sap, build.

Half-Life
      after Inger Christensen's *Alphabet*
      "cicadas, cedars, cypresses, the cerebellum."

0

1
Absolute, tender lead type, rigid press allowing this storied longing.

1
Arabic, Akkadian, English. Affinity, alikeness and attachment.

2
Before sight, before blackberries, before poetry.
Before *before*.

3
Cicadas exist, of course
their song, their center,
thrushing summer heart.

5
December approaches, early dusk, dogs flush late
departing geese, eruption of honk and wing, divided sky.
Darkness and delicate mathematics, of decimals. Diurnal
rhythms, deeply dependent on daylight & longitude.
Divided between dark or light, music or meaning?

8
Experiments exist; elk and rare earth elements;
Einsteinium exists, elk eat and are eaten,
their lives are full, not half, not volatile, decay
exists, decomposition, dogs and Dodges, rusting rails and free
electrons. Influence; magnetic fields and full hips, curve
each mountain pass, each watershed, each isotope
a carefully curving signature, place, name, coordinates
enter into alphabets, lists of the lost.

13
Fibonacci exists, dreaming in Arabic, in Pisa,
its tower not yet tilted, foundation yet to fail, Leonardo
finding spirals everywhere, ferns, pine cones, snails,
algorithms and ribbons
and finally, his Liber Abaci.
Families exist and rabbits and reproduction
& numeric place value exists, as does interest
and compounding debt and sediment. Tectonic plates
and subduction and magma exist, burden of geology, burden exists
foundations fail. Materials may be engineered, given limits
hearing fails, hearts too and dogs, dogs fail, friendships
exist, humans are animals and dogs dream. When they fail
their humans hurt. Each one twice as hard to lose as the last.

8
Great friendships exist
good dog, good dog,
grateful human, grateful human.
Animal speech exists, years exist,
so many good days compounded, emotion and mileage.
Good belly rubs and that spot just beneath the collar,
when scratched, dog smile spreads, parietal plates spread,
good dog.

5
God-given years, the flat world, given shape by
friendship, frequency of seasons and cicadas and emergence.
Every seventeen years, or is it eleven? However
erratic, each nymph, each pup, eventually
decays.

3
Dogs, deliverance.
Care and feeding. Breakup and
brothers and ice and bridges.

2
Brittle salmon bones in the wrack line. Brevity and breathlessness, brooding but not broadsided.

1
Alone but

1
alive.

0

Notes

"Her Story"
> *Mociute* is Grandmother, *Laurita* is Little/Dear Lauren, *Jonukus* is Little John (Lithuanian).

"Lesser Devils"
> *Mociute* is Grandmother, *Tevukas* is Grandfather, *Mamiete* is Mother (Lithuanian).

"Ways to Say Please"
> *Bitte, pozhaluysta, prashau* are please in German, Russian, Lithuanian. *Karoliai gintaris* is amber necklace (Lithuanian).

"Kaldunai"
> *Kaldunai* are dumplings, *rupnikas* is honey liqueur, *Dangu* is heaven, *Lietuva* is Lithuania, *Mociute* is Grandmother, *Tevukas* is Grandfather (Lithuanian). *Palmeni* is dumpling (Russian).

"Half-Life"
> After Inger Christensen's poem, *Alphabet* (*alphabet*, Danish) which uses an abecedarian form in which the number of lines in each section is dictated by the Fibonacci sequence.

Acknowledgments

This book would not exist without the support, tough-love, laughter and friendship of those closest to me, Melinda, Finn and Oscar. You three fill these pages and my life with adventure, light and meaning.

The roots of this collection took hold and found fertile ground in the hardwood forests and lakes of the Michigan of my childhood, in the rugged coastlines and mountain sanctuaries of Southeast Alaska and on the Baltic shores of Lithuania, the land of my grandparents, that came alive through memory and imagination. To all of these storied landscapes and the poems that echo their wild songs, I am grateful.

To all of my teachers, those who patiently tended to the kindling when my fire diminished to smolder and smoke, your belief billowed those fragile flames. To Peter Markus, James Glowacki and Leonard Karschnia for helping me find a way through high school by way of riding the wave of writing. To my mentors at the University of Alaska Anchorage, Zack Rogow, Ann Caston and Erin Coughlin Hollowell. Zack, you opened my eyes to so much, to Nâzım Hikmet, Lorca and Martinaitis. You held my hand and guided me away from the edge. Erin, you believed and in doing so helped me to believe in myself enough to bring the beginnings of this book to life. To others who helped in ways they will never know, Eva Saulitis, Sherry Simpson, Sherwin Bitsui, Bob Hicok and Craig Childs.

To all the poets I've been lucky to call friends, if only for too brief periods; Raquel Vazquez Gilliland, Chaun Ballard, Dan Branch, Brandon Thompson and Ann Haven McDonald. To those who I've shared a strong bond through our love of language and storied worlds; Gary Lutz, Jeremy Pataky and Aleria Jensen.

Thank you to my colleagues at the University of Alaska Southeast, your knowledge and passion contribute to a vibrant and creative community in which I am fortunate to have found meaningful work.

And lastly, to my parents, Terry and Kristina Lamb (1951-2023), for giving me the love, the time and space to find my way, in writing and in life. To my siblings, Lauren and Kevin for your steadfast belief and unconditional love from thousands of miles away. To my ancestors, in particular Antanas, Eugenia and Leonas Azelis, thank you for opening our eyes to a much bigger world, for complicating history, for your patience, stories, language and of course, kaldunai!

Thanks to the editors of these journals/projects for giving my work a space to breathe, stretch and grow.

"Small Craft Advisory" was featured in *Juneau's Poetry OmniBus* (poems on city transit).

"Betting on Longshots" and "What the Body Remembers" appeared in the 2020 edition of *Tidal Echoes*.

"Long-Range Reconnaissance" (previously titled, "Overlooked) was selected for the *49 Writers Broadside Invitational.*

John Balaban, excerpt from "Words for My Daughter" from Locusts at the Edge of Summer: New and Selected Poems. Copyright © 1991 by John Balaban. Reprinted with the permission of The Permissions Company, LLC on behalf of Copper Canyon Press, coppercanyonpress.org.

Michael Wiegers, excerpt from "Introduction" from The Poet's Child: A Copper Canyon Press Anthology Michael Wiegers, ed. Copyright © 2002 Copper Canyon Press. Reprinted with the permission of The Permissions Company, LLC on behalf of Copper Canyon Press, coppercanyonpress.org.

Joe Mills, excerpt from "How You Know" which appeared in Rattle, Vol. 16, no. 1, Summer 2010. Copyright © 2010 by Joe Mills. Reprinted by permission of Joe Mills.

Jonas Lamb is a poet, literary advocate, long-time volunteer radio host and librarian. His work has been shaped by the hard and harsh beauty of life in Southeast Alaska, his Michigan childhood, his mother's artwork and the immigrant stories of his Lithuanian grandparents. His work has appeared in *Tidal Echoes, The Kent Collector* and been featured on 360 *TV's Writers' Showcase, 49 Writers Broadside Invitational,* and *Mudrooms*. In 2017 he co-produced, *A Braided Way: Poetry, Parenting & Place,* an exhibition at the Juneau-Douglas City Museum featuring original broadside poems paired with visual art made by and in collaboration with his sons. In 2023 he served as guest judge for the Fairbanks Arts Association's 28th Statewide Poetry Contest. He received his BGS in interdisciplinary studies from the University of Michigan, his MS in Library and Information Science from Drexel University and his MFA in Poetry from the University of Alaska Anchorage. Jonas is currently a professor of library science at the University of Alaska Southeast. He lives in Juneau, Alaska with his wife and sons.

www.ingramcontent.com/pod-product-compliance
Lightning Source LLC
Chambersburg PA
CBHW020831190426
43197CB00037B/1533